CONTENTS

SEASIDE TOWNS

Seaside towns are special. They look out onto the open sea. Sometimes waves crash on the shore. Sometimes the water is calm and dotted with boats. The sound of gulls fills the salty air.

Some people live by the sea all their lives. Others choose to **retire** there. Many seaside towns are resorts, too, that people visit on holiday. The holidaymakers come to the town for a short while, but do not live there.

retire

To stop working for a living. Most people retire around the age of 65.

Most seaside towns have been lived in for hundreds of years – or even longer. Some people first settled there because they could make a living by fishing. Others came to work on the trading ships that sailed in and out, bringing goods from faraway lands.

LONG AGO

Some seaside towns have castles. Many were built during the Middle Ages, a time when there was lots of fighting in Europe. Some are even older than that.

Castles are built on high ground, with a good view of the land around. Seaside castles are often on clifftops, so they have a view of the sea, too. No attacker can get close without being seen. This is St Andrew's Castle in Fife, eastern Scotland.

Middle Ages

The time in history from around 1,000 to 500 years ago.

Some seaside towns have small, round forts called Martello towers. More than a hundred of these were built in the 1800s. This one is on the coast at Eastbourne in southern England.

PLACES TO LIVE

Like all towns, seaside towns have different kinds of homes. There are old homes and new homes, large houses and small apartments.

There may be old fishermen's cottages down by the harbour, close to the boats. There are usually tall houses, built long ago for the rich traders who brought goods from over the seas. There are grand villas, too, from **Victorian** times.

What pretty houses!

There are lots of bungalows at the seaside. Elderly people like living in bungalows because there are no stairs to climb. People take pride in their gardens. They add seaside ornaments such as anchors.

Victorian
From the time when Victoria was queen of Great Britain, from 1837 to 1901.

Seaside towns also have flats and apartments. Some are found around the marina, where all the little boats dock. They have fantastic views!

AT THE HARBOUR

Many seaside towns have a harbour or port. It is a busy place. There are lots of buildings here.

The port has offices and huge warehouses where goods are kept. There might be a market nearby, where fishermen sell their catch of the day.

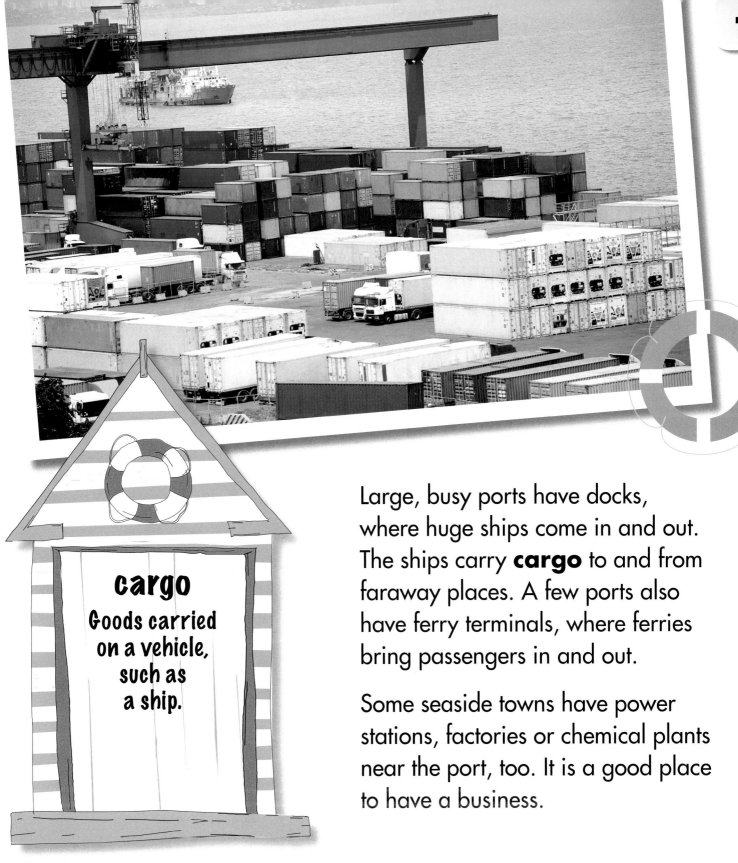

cargo
Goods carried on a vehicle, such as a ship.

Large, busy ports have docks, where huge ships come in and out. The ships carry **cargo** to and from faraway places. A few ports also have ferry terminals, where ferries bring passengers in and out.

Some seaside towns have power stations, factories or chemical plants near the port, too. It is a good place to have a business.

BEACH BUILDINGS

Seaside towns often have a beach. It might be sandy or covered in shingle (pebbles). There are special buildings on and around the beach.

Beach huts are wooden cabins. They are often pretty colours. They stand at the top of the beach, where they won't get wet at high tide. People get changed in their beach hut before they sunbathe or swim in the sea. They use the hut to store deck chairs, blankets and beach toys.

Which ice-cream do you want?

kiosk

A booth or hut that sells small items such as drinks and snacks.

There are other useful buildings on the beach. **Kiosks** sell drinks and snacks. There are public toilets and showers. Some beaches have an outdoor pool called a lido. The lido is a safer, warmer place to swim and play than the sea.

SEA SAFETY

Every town tries to keep its people safe from dangers. Seaside towns have an extra danger to think about – the sea.

Some seaside towns have a lighthouse. A lighthouse is a tower that flashes at night. It shows boat captains where the shore is. Long ago, lighthouses had a **lighthouse keeper**. These days, the light runs on its own. Now that boats have better equipment for finding the way, lighthouses are not so important. Some are used as holiday cottages instead.

Off we go!

Lifeboats are kept in the lifeboat station. Lifeboats are launched if a ship or boat is in trouble. They go to save the crew and passengers. Lifeboats also rescue swimmers who are swept out to sea.

lighthouse keeper
Someone who looks after a lighthouse and works its signals.

EATING AND DRINKING

Seaside towns have lots of different places to eat and drink. People who live in the town visit them, and so do people who are on holiday.

The seaside is famous for fish and chip shops. The fish is as fresh as can be! Some fish and chip shops only serve takeaways. Others have tables where people can sit and eat. Seaside towns have other cafés, pubs and restaurants, too.

Yummy!

knicker-bocker glory
An ice-cream dessert. Find out its ingredients on page 22.

Ice-cream parlours are a special treat at the seaside. They are cafés that serve different flavours of ice-cream. There are ice-cream desserts, such as banana splits or **knickerbocker glories**. The oldest ice-cream parlours have been been around for 70 years or more.

ON THE SEAFRONT

Many seaside towns have a pier. It is a walkway that sticks out into the sea. The first piers were made of wood. Later, iron was used and then concrete.

People visit piers to have fun. There are cafes and stalls and lots of games to play. There might even be fairground rides for children. Some seaside towns have big amusement parks with rides for all the family.

Let's go to the fairground rides.

bandstand

An outdoor platform, usually with a roof, where bands play.

Seaside towns often have very grand gardens full of roses and other beautiful flowers. Palm trees grow well in seaside towns that get a lot of sunshine. There may be parks with lovely lakes for people to stroll by and a **bandstand** where brass bands often play.

INDOOR ATTRACTIONS

Seaside towns have lots of indoor attractions. Tourists can have fun even when it's raining.

Castles, churches and grand houses are fun to visit. The Royal Pavilion in Brighton (below) was once a king's seaside home. It has beautiful rooms to explore. Many towns have museums of local history. These have **artefacts** from the sea or even fossils found on the seashore. Seaside towns often have art galleries, because many artists like to live by the sea.

artefact

An object made by people, sometimes long ago.

Old dockyards can be turned into museums. At Portsmouth's dockyard, you can explore a 200-year-old ship called HMS *Victory* (above). Some towns also have aquariums or wildlife reserves where people can find out more about sea animals.

THINGS TO DO

Now you've found out lots about seaside towns. Are you ready for a project? Here are some ideas for fantastic follow-on activities:

1. Build a castle

Find pictures of castles. The simplest ones just have a square tower called a keep. You can make one with building bricks. Make the top walls of the towers go up and down, not straight along, so archers can hide when firing their arrows.

2. Design a garden

If you were planting a new garden in a seaside park, how would you make it special? You could plant coloured flowers to make a seaside picture. Will there be places to sit or play? Draw and label your design.

3. Create a collage

Rows of beach huts make a colourful collage. Tear up old magazines and sort the scraps of paper by colour. Sketch your picture first – then get sticking! Make each beach hut a different colour.

4. Make a 'catch of the day' board

Imagine you are a fisherman selling your fish at the market. Write the names on a piece of card. Cod, haddock, crab, plaice, sea bass, skate and shrimp… can you think of others? Find or draw pictures on your card.

5. Make a knickerbocker glory

See if you can make a knickerbocker glory as delicious as the ones in ice-cream parlours. In a tall dish, layer spoonfuls of fruit in syrupy sauce with scoops of vanilla and strawberry ice-cream. Top with whipped cream, wafer biscuits and a fresh strawberry. Add a sprig of mint if you have one!

NOTES FOR ADULTS

The **Beside the Seaside** series has been carefully planned to provide an extra resource for young children, both at school and at home. It supports and extends their learning by linking to the KS1 curriculum and beyond.

In Geography, a foundation subject at this level, the seaside is a rich and popular topic because it allows children to:

1a Ask geographical questions [for example, 'What is it like to live in this place?']

1c Express their own views about people, places and environments [for example, residents and tourists, resort attractions and places to stay]

2a Use geographical vocabulary [for example, near, far, north, south, coast, cliff]

2d Use secondary sources of information [for example, CD-ROMs, pictures, photographs, stories, information texts, videos, artefacts]

3a Identify and describe what places are like [for example, in terms of landscape, jobs, weather]

3c Recognise how places have become the way they are and how they are changing [for example, the importance of the fishing industry]

3d Recognise how places compare with other places [for example, compare a seaside town to a city]

4a Make observations about where things are located [for example, a bandstand on a pier or in a public park] and about other features in the environment [for example, seasonal changes in weather]

It also provides plenty of opportunities for crossover work with other subjects.

The four titles in this series split the seaside into four sub-topics:
Seaside Holidays Then and Now
Seaside Jobs
Seaside Plants and Animals
Seaside Towns

In addition to Geography, the four books support the core subjects of English, Mathematics and Science and other foundation subjects such as Art and Design, Design and Technology and History – especially if children are encouraged to get involved in the suggested extension activities on the facing page.

Reading with children

When children are learning to read, they become more confident and make quicker progress if they are exposed to as many different types of writing as possible. In particular, their reading should not only focus on fiction and stories, but on non-fiction too. The **Beside the Seaside** books offer young readers different levels of text – for example, straightforward factual sentences and fun speech bubbles. As well as maintaining children's interest, these offer children the opportunity to distinguish between different types of communication.

Make the most of your reading time. Whether it is the adult or the child who is reading, he or she should try to follow the words with his or her fingers – this is useful for non-readers, reluctant readers and confident readers alike. Pausing in your reading gives a chance for questions and to discuss the content of the pictures. For reluctant readers, try turning the reading into a game – perhaps you read alternate pages, or the child only reads speech bubble text. To further encourage interactivity with the content, there is a small artwork of a bucket and spade hidden on every main spread for children to find.

INDEX